W9-AHY-785

J   574285
363.3   11.95
Ber
Bernards
Gun control

DATE DUE			
CC 383	4-23-93	ILL	
651	5-30-96	Sd	10211 A

✓

GREAT RIVER REGIONAL LIBRARY

St. Cloud, Minnesota 56301

Gun
Control

Look for these and other books in the Lucent
Overview series:

Acid Rain
AIDS
Animal Rights
The Beginning of Writing
Cancer
Dealing with Death
Drugs and Sports
Drug Trafficking
Eating Disorders
Endangered Species
Energy Alternatives
Extraterrestrial Life
Garbage
Gun Control
Hazardous Waste
The Holocaust
Homeless Children
Ocean Pollution
Oil Spills
The Olympic Games
Ozone
Population
Rainforests
Smoking
Special Effects in the Movies
Teen Alcoholism
The UFO Challenge
Vietnam

Gun
Control

by Neal Bernards

LUCENT
B·O·O·K·S

574285

4230603

Library of Congress Cataloging-in-Publication Data

Bernards, Neal, 1963-
    Gun control / by Neal Bernards.
        p.   cm. — (Lucent overview series)
    Includes bibliographical references and index.
    Summary: Discusses the importance of the gun in American history
and culture and the present issue of gun control in other
countries and our own.
    ISBN 1-56006-127-8
    1. Gun control—United States—Juvenile literature.   2. Firearms
ownership—United States—Juvenile literature.   [1. Gun control.
2. Firearms ownership.]   I. Title. II. Series.
HV7436.B47   1991
363.3'3'0973—dc20   91-15561

No part of this book may be reproduced or used in any form or by any means, electrical,
mechanical, or otherwise, including, but not limited to, photocopy, recording, or any
information storage and retrieval system, without prior written permission from the publisher.

© Copyright 1991 by Lucent Books, Inc.
P.O. Box 289011, San Diego, CA 92198-0011

Contents

1

The Gun Culture in America

"Firearms have long been an important part of American life. For many years the armed-citizen soldier was the country's first line of defense; the 'Kentucky' long rifle opened the frontier; the Winchester repeater 'won the West'; and the Colt revolver 'made men equal.' . . . If our frontier disappeared, our frontier tradition remains."

The Report of the National Commission on the Causes and Prevention of Violence, Task Force on Firearms and Violence

GUNS ARE AT THE VERY CORE of the American way of life. From the first settlers to present-day soldiers, firearms have played a vital role in the nation's history. The early settlers relied on guns for putting food on their tables, for protection, for taking the land they wanted to settle, and for keeping it. Colonial fighters, armed with only their muskets, held off trained British soldiers to gain the nation's independence. In the two centuries since that time, Americans have again and again turned to guns in war, in crime, in sport, and in entertainment. It seems that no other nation in the world is influenced as much by the gun as is the United States.

(opposite page) The earliest American settlers relied on guns for food and protection. Firearms were essential for surviving in a wild, new land.

This influence grew partly from frontier reality and partly from romanticized mythology. The early settlers could not have survived conditions in the harsh New World without guns. Like plows and axes, guns were essential tools for making the new land a productive home. Unlike the plow and ax, however, guns attained an almost legendary status.

Harold F. Williamson, in his history of the Winchester rifle, writes, "Firearms, the axe, and the plow were the three cornerstones upon which the pioneer Americans built this nation. Of the three, firearms were the most dramatic and appealed most to popular imagination." Possibly this is because the ax and the plow symbolized the sweat and hard work required for building a new nation. Guns, on the other hand, represented swift and lethal power. With the pull of a trigger and a well-aimed shot, pioneers could kill a bounding buck for the family table or ward off attackers. Reliable, accurate muskets therefore became possessions of pride. And the men and women who used them came to be viewed by many as heroes and adventurers. Colonial sol-

European settlers disembark from their ship to begin life in the New World. They came armed with muskets for protection against unknown dangers.

diers, Kentucky riflemen, explorers, western settlers, and lawmen throughout U.S. history raised the gun's reputation to mythic levels.

The American attitude toward guns began with the arrival of colonists in the New World. They brought with them muzzle-loading muskets and large, clumsy guns used to hunt game on the open fields of Europe. These guns were often ill suited for use in a new land filled with dense woods, rolling hills, and treacherous rivers. The colonists were equally unprepared to use guns. Most of the colonists came from Great Britain, where only the wealthy owned guns and used them mainly for sport. Upon arrival in the New World, however, the colonists realized that the skilled use of lead bullets and gunpowder as ammunition would be essential for their survival. As the years passed and settlements grew, colonists became more skilled at using their guns. Eventually, they built smaller, lighter muskets that were better suited for tracking game and hunting in forests.

Wits and weapons

Settlers quickly learned that the New World differed from Great Britain, even from the rest of Europe. On the northeastern coast of America where they first lived, no open fields lay waiting for crops to be sowed. No animals had been domesticated for human use. And unlike Marco Polo's journeys in the Far East, the colonists encountered no abundance of gold and silk for trading. The riches found by explorers in other parts of the world did not seem to exist in the New World. Instead, the settlers had to rely on their wits and their weapons to make a living. Frank T. Morn, a criminal justice professor at the University of Illinois-Chicago, writes that "the new land . . . was a hostile place, and guns were not a luxury of the few but a necessity for many."

An engraving portrays a colonial family fleeing an Indian attack. The gun gave settlers an advantage over Indians in many of these clashes.

Survival, the colonists realized, meant more than putting food on the table. To establish a thriving community, the colonists knew they would have to find sources of steady income. For this, they looked to their surroundings. There they saw ample numbers of wild animals that could be sold to markets in Europe for hides, feathers, and other necessities. They relied on their guns for this purpose and success soon followed.

Despite this success, life in the New World was fraught with danger. Guns became the constant companions of most settlers. They looked to their guns for protection from animal attack and to settle disputes and drunken fights with other settlers. In addition, as the settlers moved farther west, they clashed often with Native Americans, whom they called Indians. Some Indians fought the settlers because they simply resented the presence of these new people on their land. Others responded with violence only after seeing their hunting grounds invaded and their people massacred. Whatever their reasons, the Indians could not overpower the settlers' guns with their own clubs and arrows. Settlements of colonists grew and expanded farther and farther to the west. And guns cleared the way for this expansion.

As the settlements expanded, colonists began to combine their communities into an independent nation in hopes of breaking free from British rule. The British government resisted this movement and war broke out. With their superior knowledge of the land and their expert shooting skill, the colonists won. The victory of colonialist fighters over a much more powerful British army

An engraving of the Battle of Lexington during the American Revolution depicts citizen-soldiers exchanging fire with trained British soldiers. The colonists' skill with firearms and their knowledge of the terrain gave them an edge over the British.

during the Revolutionary War convinced Americans that guns were a key, not only to survival, but to freedom. "Freedom from Great Britain was not won by supermen using super weapons; it was won by ordinary citizens whose will to fight for liberty was backed by an intimate knowledge of firearms gained through the use of personal weapons," writes author James B. Trefethen in his book *Americans and Their Guns.*

Reliance on citizen soldiers

Guns alone could not achieve the colonists' freedom, however. For this, the settlers came to depend on citizen soldiers. A standing army with thousands of full-time soldiers simply was not possible. Struggling settlements could not afford to have able-bodied settlers standing guard all day. They needed people to work. So a new idea evolved. Everyone would be responsible for the community's defense. Settlers carried guns to the fields, to work, and even to church. Thus, the idea of an armed citizenry was born. It was this armed citizenry that ultimately won the nation's independence.

The astounding success of the American colonists during the Revolutionary War strengthened the idea in other countries that armed citizen soldiers could defend their own nation. This concept had never been proven to work before. Previously, world leaders had kept full-time armies at the ready to defend their nations or expand their power. Maintaining a citizen army was a radical concept. Common citizens had rarely, if ever, been entrusted with so many weapons. Most rulers preferred to keep weapons under tight control out of fear of overthrow by their subjects. And here was a nation consisting entirely of armed citizens. This idea was so widely revered in the new United

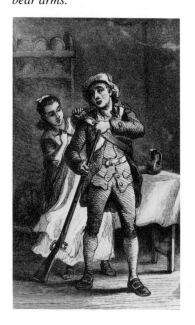

A colonist's daughter prepares him for battle. American revolutionaries learned to equate freedom with the right to bear arms.

An engraving depicts the Battle of New Orleans during the War of 1812 against Great Britain. A series of wars throughout the eighteenth and nineteenth centuries ensured the close relationship between Americans and guns.

States that it was written into the Constitution. The Second Amendment to the U.S. Constitution states that citizens have the right to keep and bear arms in the defense of the nation.

Through a series of wars, guns continued to play a part in the new nation's expansion and survival. The War of 1812, fought against the British; the Indian wars; the war with Mexico; and the Civil War all ensured that Americans kept weapons by their sides for many decades.

Settling disputes

By the early 1800s, guns had become so much a part of daily life in the United States that they were viewed as the ultimate arbiter in personal disputes. Especially in the southeastern states, many learned and respected men resolved their disagreements and defended their honor with organized gunfights called duels. These duels were conducted in a very orderly fashion according to established rules. Some duels were fought to the death. Others were not. Those who won duels

American statesmen Alexander Hamilton (left) and Aaron Burr dueled with pistols in 1804. Burr fatally wounded Hamilton in this "affair of honor."

wore their victories like badges of distinction. Winners gained new status in the community. Many duels became public spectacles where observers lined the dueling fields to watch the outcome.

Dueling was not only tolerated by government officials, but was also practiced by many, including federally elected officials. In one famous duel, U.S. vice president Aaron Burr and former secretary of the treasury Alexander Hamilton faced off in Weehawkun, New Jersey. In a political campaign for the presidency, Hamilton had so criticized Burr's abilities and personality that Burr sought to defend his honor by dueling with Hamilton. Historians do not know exactly what Hamilton said to incur Burr's wrath. Whatever it was, it so infuriated Burr that he forced Hamilton into fighting a duel on July 12, 1804. Hamilton, who did not really want to duel in the first place, purposely fired wide but Burr's shot found its mark. Hamilton died the next day from a single gunshot wound in the chest. No charges were filed against Burr and only a few people called for an end to dueling. In fact, dueling did not die out until the mid-nineteenth century, when most states finally abolished the practice.

A flood of guns

Firearms again became a centerpiece of American life in 1861. Americans took up arms—this time against each other—in what would be the nation's bloodiest war. The Civil War stemmed from a division between the industrial North and the agricultural South over slavery and other issues. Eleven southern states had announced their intention to withdraw from the country, often called the Union in those days. President Abraham Lincoln and his cabinet would not stand for a dissolution of the United States. As always, Americans looked to their guns to solve the problem. Among the many results of four years at war was an even stronger appetite for new and better firearms.

The Civil War introduced Americans to repeating rifles, which had greater range and increased killing power. Repeating rifles could fire off dozens of shots in the time it took a soldier to reload an outdated musket. Despite the threat posed by these new firearms, union leaders did not disarm most former Confederate, or southern, soldiers after the war. Disarming them apparently was viewed as too harsh a punishment. Americans, especially in rural areas, still depended on guns for personal protection and for their meals. Confiscating the gun of even a defeated soldier was considered the ultimate indignity. For this reason, Union soldiers did not take guns away from their former enemies.

Following the war, the general American populace was extremely well armed. The wartime

Abraham Lincoln was U.S. president during the Civil War. Americans were armed with many new and more precise weapons in the bloody War Between the States. Lincoln himself died in 1865 of a gunshot wound from an assassin's pistol.

surplus flooded post-Civil War society with high-quality, low-cost weapons. Among these was the Colt .45 revolver. Called "the Equalizer" because almost anyone could use it, the Colt .45 had become a popular weapon in the West, especially in Texas, during the 1840s. The Texas Rangers, whose task was enforcing the law, needed a lightweight, fast, and reliable weapon to help patrol the state. The Colt .45 was easier to carry on horseback and more accessible during surprise attacks than rifles. During range wars between ranchers, battles with Indians, and the Mexican-American War, Texans discovered that this well-designed six-shooter saved them many times when their rifles were out of reach. Because of the gun's success in Texas, thousands of Colts were manufactured for use in the Civil War. After the war, the surplus six-shooters fell into settlers' hands and helped them maintain control of their land. This gun's popularity reinforced the notion that guns were necessary to settle the new frontier.

Romance of the frontier

To many people living in the eastern United States around the turn of the century, frontier life seemed rugged and romantic. Guns had attained a central place in western folklore. Newspapers carried stories of outlaws, gunfighters, and cowboys. Travelers told tales of frontier shoot-outs and of men and women who carried guns as naturally as city dwellers carried umbrellas.

Along with these accounts of gunslinging derring-do, Wild West traveling shows presented exhibitions of shooting expertise that captivated East Coast audiences. The gun manufacturer Remington Arms sponsored traveling shows by sharpshooters like Annie Oakley and Frank Butler. Eastern city dwellers, most of whom had

The pinpoint accuracy of Annie Oakley and other sharpshooters raised shooting to an art and made it a legendary part of the Old West.

long since put down their guns, were astounded by the shooters' precision and skill. A good sharpshooter could hit hundreds of wooden blocks or glass balls tossed in the air without missing one. These Wild West shows introduced guns and marksmanship to new audiences across the nation, who saw none of the actual hardships of frontier life.

By the 1890s, popular magazines and novels were carrying stories of gunslinging westerners who fought ruthless bandits, shot buffalo, and drove off attackers with their trusty Winchesters and Colt .45s. These publications came to be known as pulp fiction because they were printed

A nineteenth-century advertisement praises the accuracy and durability of a variety of guns.

Chicago gangster Al Capone and his mob battled for control of organized crime during the 1920s. Mobsters popularized the use of submachine guns as the weapon of choice among criminals during the Prohibition Era.

on cheap pulp paper. Pulp fiction gave everyday people a taste of the West. The pages were filled with exciting stories of quick-drawing, good-guy sheriffs protecting innocent town folk from gun-wielding outlaws. They told tales of cowboys roaming the dusty range, shooting varmints and rustlers who threatened to harm their cattle. Edward F. Dolan, Jr., the author of *Gun Control,* describes the pulp-fiction hero as having "all the traits that we Americans like. He was independent-minded. He was fearless. Strong. Determined. And, above all, he was a man of action, a man who overcame danger, righted wrongs, and brought the law to a wild frontier."

Creating legends

Even gun-toting, violent outlaws like Billy the Kid were romanticized in pulp fiction. While most modern historians consider Billy the Kid a troubled loner and psychopath, the stories of the day portrayed him as a daring renegade. In 1881, written accounts of his exploits as a murderer and robber sold well and helped create a legend about him. Paul Trachtman, in *The Gunfighters,* writes, "Billy came off with a lurid and lasting reputation. Newspapers the country over reported his exploits while he lived, and within 10 months of his death, no fewer than eight novels were published romanticizing his career." Even his killer, Lincoln County, New Mexico sheriff Pat Garrett, publicized Billy's exploits by writing an exaggerated, inaccurate book called *An Authentic Life of Billy the Kid* shortly after the outlaw's death. Books like these reinforced the image that the West was filled with gun-wielding outlaws who set their own rules. The stories created an image of adventure and excitement for guns and gunplay.

The American public's fascination with guns

continued into Prohibition and the Depression years. Prohibition, which lasted from 1920 to 1933, was a time when alcohol could not be legally bought or sold. This era gave rise to famous gangsters like Al Capone and John Dillinger. Capone supplied bootleg, or illegal, liquor to those Americans who still wanted to drink alcohol. He and his Chicago gang fought violent "wars" with other gangs in hopes of cornering the market on illegal liquor. Dillinger was a bank robber known for his expert use of a Thompson submachine gun, also known as a tommy gun. Their gun battles were chronicled in gory detail by the nation's newspapers. Readers were both repulsed and fascinated by the gunfights detailed in the gangster stories. Together with their guns, some of these gangsters came to be seen as larger than life.

A symbol of the nation's strength

World War II interrupted the attention lavished on gun-toting gangsters and focused it instead on Germany's march through Europe. The war did not lessen the American fascination with guns. If anything, interest grew because American guns were being put to heroic use. American soldiers armed with M-1 rifles were fighting the Germans, Italians, and Japanese. The public saw the troops as protecting democracy with their guns just as their forebears had done in earlier wars. "Once again the gun became the symbol of the nation's strength," write Lee Kennett and James LaVerne Anderson in *The Gun in America.*

Many American soldiers returning from World War II brought home souvenir weapons like German Lugers, Italian Berettas, and British Enfield rifles. This influx of weapons after World War II marked the beginning of gun collecting as a widespread hobby in the United States. The necessity of beating back the frontier, warding off robbers, or killing gangsters with guns had passed. But the pleasure and pride of owning guns grew.

Popular pastimes

Another tradition of American life, hunting, expanded in popularity after World War II. Some people still hunted animals such as deer, ducks, and rabbits because they needed food. But most simply enjoyed hunting as sport. People were drawn to hunting by the chance to test their skills and wit. Hunting gave people a reason to be out-of-doors and closer to the natural environment that had grown distant with the rise of cities. It reminded people of a time that seemed less complicated. Hunting today remains one of the nation's most popular participant sports. About twenty million Americans hunt every year, spending more than $8 billion annually on their hobby.

Guns also provided recreation of another sort. In the 1950s and 1960s, Westerns on television took viewers back to a time of gunslinging adventures on the American frontier. Series like "Gunsmoke," "Have Gun Will Travel," and "The Rifleman" filled American screens with images of rugged men and women surviving in a nearly lawless West with the help of rifles and six-shooters. Millions of families avidly watched dusty cowboys and lawmen triumph over evil with their rifles and sidearm handguns. The programs represented the nation's bold and harsh pioneering past when gunslingers freely roamed the land and every citizen carried a gun at all times. For some viewers, the Westerns offered a sense of adventure that seemed to be missing in everyday life.

By the 1970s Westerns gave way to detective

and police stories. In these television shows and movies, justice was meted out not by cowboys and small-town sheriffs with Winchester rifles and Colt .45s, but by hard-nosed urban police officers with .38 Specials and .44 Magnums. Then, in the 1980s, the crime-fighting team of Sonny Crockett and Rico Tubbs leveled their Uzis and repeating pistols at drug traffickers on "Miami Vice." In the late 1980s Rambo appeared in motion pictures with a monstrous machine gun that could destroy a gas station. And in the 1990s, superheroes like those played by Arnold Schwarzenegger use futuristic weapons with laser-guided sights and exploding ammunition rounds to vanquish their foes. Cinematic weaponry is so common that experienced filmgoers have become familiar with gun terms like M-16, AK-47, and Mac-10.

Modern-day movie heroes like Arnold Schwarzenegger use sophisticated, high-tech weapons to vanquish their enemies in today's action movies.

The ties that bind

Americans and guns have a unique relationship. This relationship started with the arrival of the first pilgrims and continues to this day. No other industrialized nation is so fond of guns, or gives them such a prominent place in its culture. Many Americans retain a deep-seated belief in individual liberty and the right to protect themselves and their country through the use of guns.

Guns continue to be a part of everyday life in the United States. History books, television shows, movies, and the nation's recreation all resound with the echo of gunfire. With guns at the core of their society, it is not surprising that Americans have such difficulty reaching agreement on gun control.

2

Approaches to Gun Control

GUN CONTROL IN THE United States is guided by a patchwork of federal, state, and local laws. These laws, estimated to number more than twenty thousand, take many different approaches to controlling the sales, ownership, and use of guns. Most gun control measures in the United States are directed at handguns. Handguns are small, powerful, relatively cheap, easy to use, and accurate only at short distances. They can be easily hidden in a pocket, under a jacket, or in a car. For this reason, and because they can be fired by one hand, handguns are popular for both crime and personal protection. Though they can be used for hunting and target shooting, their main purpose is for shooting people.

Tracking the numbers

Because the United States has no single system for registering firearm ownership, it is difficult to know exactly how many guns are owned by private citizens. Estimates range from 150 million to 175 million. It is also difficult to know exactly how many of these are handguns. The government agency in charge of enforcing federal gun control laws, the Bureau of Alcohol, Tobacco, and Firearms (BATF), estimates that 52 million

(opposite page) A Florida gun seller demonstrates the correct use of a Smith & Wesson .357 Magnum pistol to a prospective buyer. Most gun control laws are aimed at over-the-counter sales.

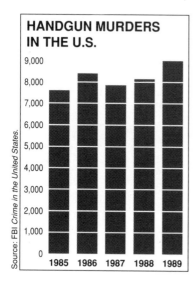

HANDGUN MURDERS IN THE U.S.

9,000
8,000
7,000
6,000
5,000
4,000
3,000
2,000
1,000
0

1985 1986 1987 1988 1989

Source: FBI *Crime in the United States.*

handguns are circulating in the United States and about 2 million more are bought each year. According to *Fortune* magazine, weapons manufacturers in the United States alone made 1.99 million handguns in 1989.

No one really knows how many handguns are bought to commit crimes and how many are bought for personal protection. But statistics from various sources can provide background for understanding the place of handguns in American society today. Approximately 43 percent of all murders in the United States in 1987 were committed with handguns, according to statistics from the Federal Bureau of Investigation (FBI). The BATF estimates that handguns are involved in 71 percent of all armed crimes. Of the twelve thousand people who commit suicide each year in the United States, nearly 60 percent of them use handguns. And according to *U.S. News & World Report*, there were 1,501 accidental shooting deaths in 1988. Handguns were probably involved in about one-fourth of those accidents. These numbers have led some people to conclude that handguns are a menace to society.

For these reasons, handguns—as opposed to hunting guns and other guns commonly used for sport—have been the focus of most gun control laws. In recent years, however, another category of guns has come to the public's attention. These guns, called assault rifles, have also been targeted as needing regulation. Military-style assault rifles are generally described as semiautomatic rifles that can easily be converted so that they are fully automatic, or rapid-firing.

Reaching beyond regional boundaries

For the most part, gun control in the United States has been viewed as a matter for local and state legislators. This has resulted in widely differing approaches to gun control. In rural areas, researchers have found, gun control appears to be less common than in more urban areas, for example. According to the authors of *The Citizen's Guide to Gun Control*, 33 percent of eastern households own guns, while 50 percent of the rest of the nation's households own guns. This disparity may account for differing gun laws between the regions. Despite the regional differences, however, the nation's most significant gun control laws are federal laws.

Two laws passed in the 1930s were created in response to the wave of violence that accompanied Prohibition and the rise of gangsters. The 1934 National Firearms Act was passed to make it more difficult for gangsters to get guns, such as machine guns and sawed-off shotguns. Gangsters preferred these guns because they were efficient and intimidating. The firearms act placed heavy taxes on all aspects of making, distributing, and registering these guns. The 1938 Federal Fire-

A prospective buyer gets the feel of a handgun at a gun store. The federal government estimates that two million handguns are sold each year in the United States.

Most gun control advocates seek to ban, limit the sale of, or limit the possession of Saturday Night Specials—small, cheap handguns most often used in weekend violence.

arms Act prohibited the buying and selling of firearms across state lines except by federally licensed gun dealers. This law also made it illegal to sell guns to felons.

However, the Federal Firearms Act was repealed in 1968. In its place came the Gun Control Act of 1968. This law blocks minors, felons, and mentally ill people from owning guns. It bans the private ownership of military-type weapons such as bazookas, machine guns, mortars, grenade launchers, and artillery guns. In addition, it prohibits other countries from selling handguns known as "Saturday Night Specials" in the United States. Most of these guns were manufactured in other countries and then sold in the United States. Some legislators viewed this prohibition as a means of limiting their numbers and, in turn, possibly reducing crime. These handguns got their name from police in Detroit, Michigan, who found them to be cheap, small, inaccurate, and most commonly used in weekend violence. The Gun Control Act also requires gun dealers to be licensed by the federal government. This act remains the most comprehensive law governing weapons' ownership in the United States today.

Many cities and states have passed their own gun control laws since that time. These laws attempt to control guns in a variety of ways, including registration, waiting periods, permits, bans, and combinations of these strategies. It is difficult to evaluate how well these various forms of gun control work. But the experiences of specific cities and states can provide some insight into why these approaches were adopted and how well they have worked in those locations.

Registering guns

Registration is a commonly discussed form of gun control, yet it is used in relatively few places. In 1987 only six states—Hawaii, Illinois, Kansas, Michigan, Mississippi, and New York—and the District of Columbia required handgun registration of any kind. Of those, Illinois and Kansas required handgun registration only in some cities and counties.

To register a handgun, gun buyers usually provide their name and address, the type of weapon they are buying, and its serial number to the gun

© Steve Turtil/Rothco. Reprinted with permission.

shop owner. In some states, gun shops keep this information in their files. In other states, this information is maintained by police. Gun registration works much like car registration. When a person buys a car, the buyer must provide the state with his or her name, address, the type of car being purchased, and its identification number. This information is kept on record with state and local authorities.

The goal of registration is twofold. It aims to hold gun owners accountable for their weapons, and it provides police with a starting point for investigations when guns are used to commit crimes. Just as police can trace a car to its registered owner when an accident occurs, police can trace a gun to its registered owner when it is involved in a crime. Police can then talk to the gun owner to find if he or she was involved in the crime. Gun registration does not limit a person's ability to buy a gun, as do some other methods of gun control. It serves only as an information system, mostly to be used by police during crime investigations.

Useful or wasteful?

Gun registration has its critics and its supporters. Critics say registration is a waste of time because it offers many opportunities for fraud. A gun buyer can register under a false name and address or let this information lapse when moving to a new address. Others argue that criminals, who often get guns illegally anyway, are unlikely to register their guns. This would leave a large group of guns unaccounted for, rendering the system useless. Alan Gottlieb, the chairman of the Citizen's Committee for the Right to Keep and Bear Arms, writes, "Gun registration is not needed. It doesn't do anything useful. It doesn't help trace criminals for the simple reason that

Sargent © 1989 *Austin American-Statesman.* Reprinted with permission of Universal Press Syndicate. All rights reserved.

criminals don't register their guns." Critics also say the government has no more right to require personal information from gun buyers than it does from owners of other items. Knives are sometimes used in violent crimes, for example, yet the government does not require consumers to register their knives. Some gun owners also fear misuse of registration information, which they say could someday be used to confiscate guns belonging to all private citizens.

Supporters of gun registration, on the other hand, say the biggest problem with this idea is that it is not now being followed nationwide. No national computer system currently exists to record and track ownership information. As long as one city or state requires registration and a neighboring city or state does not, registration cannot really be effective. Luis Tolley, the western director of Handgun Control, Inc. (HCI), an organization in favor of gun control, says, "As long as criminals can simply walk into gun stores in neighboring states and smuggle weapons into [a state with registration], we won't be safe."

Many more cities and states require gun buyers to obtain permits before buying a gun than require registration. Permits can take many different forms. As of 1987, at least thirteen states required handgun permits, according to the National Rifle Association (NRA), an organization that opposes gun control. Twenty-nine states required permits to openly carry handguns. Thirty-three states required a permit to carry a concealed weapon. Some cities and states also require different permits to carry a handgun in one's car or to keep it at one's place of business. Unlike registration, which is more a formality than a screening tool, permits limit access to firearms since only those who receive permits may legally buy guns.

Obtaining a permit

To obtain a permit, a potential gun buyer must agree to a background check. Background checks are done in varying degrees of detail and may take only a few moments or several weeks. Permits typically are withheld from those with criminal records or a history of mental illness. Some agencies use fingerprints; others use computers or both for checking a person's background. Police officials in Atlanta, Georgia, for example, use a potential buyer's fingerprints to check background. Through the permit process, Atlanta officials say, they have found that 10 percent of all potential handgun buyers lied about their criminal or mental health records.

The permit process attempts to screen handgun buyers to make certain they have a legitimate need for a handgun. Typically, potential gun buyers apply directly to local police departments for a permit. Some laws limit handgun ownership to people who use them in their work. This category might include security guards, private detectives, and bodyguards. Celebrities, politicians, business leaders, and other prominent citizens sometimes

can obtain permits by demonstrating that their public status makes them a likely target for armed attack. Authorities then check the applicant's background and either accept or reject the request on the basis of these criteria.

A useful tool

Some people worry about giving local authorities the power to determine who can own a handgun. Alan Gottlieb believes permit systems discriminate against many people. Unless one is a celebrity or a well-known politician, he and others say, the chances of getting a gun permit are small. "Virtually every place where permit laws are in place, it is either impossible or impractical for ordinary citizens to get gun permits," Gottlieb writes.

Others view permits as a useful tool. As with registration, permits enable police to trace handguns to their owners. Permits also weed out some

A Philadelphia policeman practices with an Austrian-made Glock 17 semiautomatic pistol, a deadlier weapon than the .38 caliber sidearm traditionally issued to police officers. Some gun laws limit ownership of handguns to police officers, security guards, and other persons who use them in their work.

applicants whom the law bans from gun ownership. When the permit process stretches over a period of days or even weeks, as it does in some communities, it can also discourage purchases made in haste or anger. This last element makes up the core of another form of gun control known as a waiting or cooling-off period.

Making people wait

Waiting periods are designed primarily to keep someone from buying and using a gun in a fit of anger. Statistics show that handguns frequently are fired during passionate and angry exchanges between people who know each other. A waiting period provides time for anger to subside. During this time, some people say, anger may cool and the potential buyer may decide not to buy a gun, or at least not use it. Many communities also use waiting periods for background checks on potential buyers.

At least twenty states have adopted waiting periods as a form of gun control. The waits vary in length. Alabama requires a two-day wait, while New York's waiting period can last three months or more.

Waiting periods also have their critics and their supporters. Critics say waiting periods have done little to reduce crimes committed in anger. Nor can they be counted on to weed out persons with a history of mental illness or emotional instability, these critics contend. John Hinckley, who tried to assassinate President Ronald Reagan in 1981, legally purchased his handgun in Texas despite being emotionally unbalanced. Although Texas did not have a waiting period, a waiting period probably would not have prevented Hinckley from getting a gun, critics say. This is because Hinckley had never been institutionalized for mental illness and had no criminal record. And

Would-be presidential assassin John Hinckley Jr., bound in chains and wearing a bulletproof vest, is escorted by federal officers to a security cell. Critics argue that stricter gun laws would not have prevented Hinckley from buying a gun.

because Hinckley apparently did not shoot President Reagan in a fit of anger, a cooling-off period probably would not have mattered. Background checks conducted during waiting periods, like permits and registration, are also subject to fraud. Those who cannot legally buy a gun can get around these measures simply by having a friend with a clean record buy the gun for them, says Jack Oglesby of High Bridge Arms, Inc. in San Francisco.

Waiting periods are viewed by some people as little more than an inconvenience to law-abiding gun buyers and an ineffective tool for halting crime. Those who are inclined to use guns for committing crimes will get guns, critics say, if not legally, then illegally. "The bottom line,"

Federal agents subdue John Hinckley Jr. (background) after he shot President Ronald Reagan on March 30, 1981. Other agents tend to a police officer (left) and presidential press secretary James Brady (right), wounded by the assailant's gunfire. Hinckley legally bought his gun in Texas. He had no record of mental illness or criminal conduct.

writes Trey Hodgkins, a spokesperson for the NRA, "is that waiting periods do not prevent criminals from getting firearms and they don't stop violent crime or slow it down."

Where they have been tried, waiting periods have drawn mixed reviews. Police officials in Columbus, Georgia, say their city's three-day waiting period and background check for handgun buyers has been extremely effective. "We catch two people a week with felony convictions [trying to buy handguns]," says Columbus's police chief.

Lengthening the wait

California has had a waiting period for handgun purchases in effect since 1953. The initial three-day wait was lengthened to fifteen days in 1975. In 1991, state legislators added waiting periods for semiautomatic rifles and pump-action shotguns. California authorities use the waiting period to conduct background checks. Of the 2.6

Jerry Barnett/*The Indianapolis News.* Reprinted with permission.

million applications made for handguns since 1982, more than 14,000 were rejected because of an applicant's criminal past or history of mental illness, according to 1991 California Department of Justice figures. This amounts to less than 1 percent of the total.

Many people are unimpressed by these numbers. They contend that such a small percentage does not justify the inconvenience to law-abiding gun buyers who must wait for the cooling-off period to end before obtaining their guns. But others say the wait is worthwhile if even a small number of people are denied guns because of criminal history or mental illness. "To these people who pooh-pooh less than 1 percent as too small a number, I say that one criminal walking into a gun store and legally buying a gun is too much," says Gwen Fitzgerald, a spokesperson for HCI.

The state of Indiana also has a waiting period. Indiana State Police statistics show that handgun applications tripled between 1987 and 1990 to 90,235. Rejections did not increase at a similar rate, however. State authorities rejected 55 applications in 1987 and 56 in 1990. That figure represents less than one-tenth of 1 percent of applicants being turned down. Again, critics say this demonstrates the ineffectiveness of waiting periods and background checks.

Keeping guns from criminals

Yet, at least one police organization remains firmly behind these measures. The Fraternal Order of Police, which represents 200,000 police officers across the nation, believes that waiting periods and background checks can keep guns from falling into the hands of criminals. "No one claims gun control will stop all gun-related crime," the organization's president, Dewey Stokes, said in 1989. "But a survey found that 28 percent of prison inmates said they had bought firearms over the counter. Stopping 28 percent of crime would be significant."

Resorting to bans

Possibly the most drastic approach to gun control is a ban on owning guns. Aside from the decades-old federal ban on private ownership of machine guns and sawed-off shotguns, few cities and states have resorted to outright bans. Where bans have been adopted, they have targeted handguns and semiautomatic rifles. This is because these guns are considered more dangerous to human life and have little use in sport or recreational activities. California and New Jersey have banned assault rifles, for example, and two Illinois cities, Chicago and Morton Grove, have banned handguns.

Bans represent an effort to remove certain firearms from general circulation and often are adopted in response to fears of growing violent crime. While nearly all gun control measures have their proponents and opponents, gun bans are probably the most controversial of these measures. Although permits and waiting periods attempt to keep certain individuals from owning guns, they do not completely outlaw those guns. Bans, on the other hand, generally try to do just that. This strikes at the heart of what some people consider their fundamental rights. They view a ban as an attempt to undermine and regulate personal decision making and choice of life-style.

One city in which officials opted for a ban was Morton Grove, Illinois, a Chicago suburb of about twenty-four thousand people. The city's 1981 ban prohibits all citizens—except police and others who use handguns in their line of work—from buying, selling, or owning handguns within city limits.

A Massachusetts gunshop owner displays a German-made semiautomatic assault rifle. California and New Jersey have banned the sale of such weapons.

The Morton Grove City Council adopted the ban for two main reasons. Council members wanted to block the planned opening of a gun store near a local junior high school, and they wanted to register a protest against violent crime. City councilman and ban sponsor Neil Cashman said at the time that community leaders needed to take a stand against handguns and gun violence. The highly publicized and controversial ban has been challenged in court numerous times, but it still stands.

A statewide ban

One of the few states to initiate a statewide ban is California. The state's landmark law prohibits the manufacture, distribution, sale, or trade of nearly sixty types of semiautomatic rifles and handguns in California. The law went into effect on January 1, 1990, and gave California residents one year to register banned guns with the state. According to state officials, 42,809 assault weapons were registered by the end of the year-long registration period on December 31, 1990. No one knows for certain how many assault weapons are privately owned in California. Some estimate the total at around 300,000. By law, police can confiscate unregistered guns.

Some people have applauded the state's action, saying the law may become a model for others to follow. Others have criticized it, saying it represents one of the most severe attacks yet on individual freedoms.

The California law was prompted by a shooting spree that left five schoolchildren dead and twenty-nine others wounded. This tragedy occurred in 1989 in Stockton, California. The gunman, Patrick Purdy, killed himself after shooting the children with an AK-47 assault rifle. Purdy had a criminal record but had legally purchased his rifle in Oregon. At the time, Oregon had a handgun waiting period but no restrictions on assault rifles. The shooting enraged many Californians. In response to public outcry, state legislators passed the ban.

Mandatory prison sentences

Some people also consider stiff or automatic prison sentences for gun-related crimes another form of gun control. The federal government and numerous state and local authorities have adopted automatic or mandatory prison sentences in an effort to deter gun-related crime. Under mandatory sentencing laws, those who commit crimes using guns or carry them unlawfully generally receive an automatic, preset prison sentence. They do not have a chance to bargain for less time in prison or for other types of punishment. Mandatory prison sentences are probably the least controversial of all the gun control measures. Some people oppose them, however, because they make no allowances for an individual's personal circum-

Bob Dix, *Manchester Union Leader.* Reprinted with permission.

stances. A first-time offender and a multiple, repeat offender could receive the same mandatory sentence if both used a gun in the same type of crime, for example.

Authorities in some cities and states have found the best approach to gun control is to combine various measures. This is the approach recommended by the International Association of Chiefs of Police. This organization, which represented fourteen thousand police chiefs in 1990, favors a combination of gun control measures for reducing crime.

The organization recommends a cooling-off period, fingerprint and criminal record checks for all potential gun buyers, positive identification of the prospective buyer or permit applicant, a photograph identification card for all approved handgun buyers, and mandatory prison sentences for persons convicted of crimes involving handguns.

State and local gun control laws continue to change across the nation. Citizens, police, and legislators continue to look for the best way to balance the desire to own guns with the responsibility of ensuring public safety. The guiding force of these laws is the Second Amendment to the U.S. Constitution.

3

The Second Amendment and Gun Control

THE SECOND AMENDMENT to the Constitution of the United States reads: "A well-regulated militia being necessary to the security of a free state, the right of the people to keep and bear arms shall not be infringed." This seemingly simple statement has sparked two centuries of argument between people who believe the government has a constitutional right to control guns and those who believe it does not.

The Second Amendment lies at the heart of the gun control debate, both because of what it says and because it is the only reference to gun possession in the Constitution. People who favor gun control and people who oppose it both believe this twenty-seven-word sentence supports their positions. This occurs because people interpret the Second Amendment differently. Gun control supporters essentially believe the Second Amendment guarantees only the right of the government to arm its militia. Gun control opponents essentially believe the Second Amendment guarantees the right of private citizens to own guns. These

(opposite page) The Bill of Rights guarantees to American citizens certain civil rights, including the right to keep and bear arms.

differences in understanding the same words arise because of the difficulty of interpreting and applying to today a statement conceived more than two hundred years ago.

The birth of the Second Amendment

The Second Amendment was born at a time when the United States was young and democracy was being tried on a large scale for the first time. After 170 years of increasingly oppressive British control, early American leaders wanted to ensure that their federal government would never become too powerful. They had already suffered under the government of King George III. King George, Britain's leader at the time of the Revolution, had been a tyrannical monarch during his reign.

Many of the American colonists objected to George's rule because he imposed taxes on the colonists without allowing them a voice in government. Colonists also had to endure the presence of British troops in their villages and cities. The sight of these soldiers on their land irritated them. With the creation of their own new government, early American legislators wanted to make sure that no one person or central government ever had such total power over their lives again. The Constitution was written to address these fears.

When the nation's founders gathered in 1787 in Philadelphia to sign the Constitution, many legislators worried that the document provided too much power to the new federal government and offered too little protection for the rights of individual citizens. It was this concern that led to the adoption in 1789 of ten constitutional amendments known as the Bill of Rights. These amendments further guaranteed various rights such as trial by jury, freedom of speech, and freedom of

The Second Amendment was included in the Bill of Rights to guarantee Americans their right to defend themselves against tyrannical rulers, such as Great Britain's King George III.

religion. The second of these amendments, the one that guarantees "the right of the people to keep and bear arms," sought to eliminate fears of vulnerability to outside attack or overthrow of the government. If every citizen were armed and ready to defend the new nation, the founders thought, it would be much less vulnerable to such threats. For this reason, the nation's founders called on citizens to arm themselves and built a provision into the Bill of Rights saying as much. This would enable citizens to defend themselves and their country whenever the need arose.

An engraving depicts the ratification of the Bill of Rights, the first ten amendments to the U.S. Constitution. The Bill of Rights was an outstanding achievement that continues to inspire other nations.

The citizen militia

Daniel Abrams, a Columbia University Law School student in New York who has closely studied the Second Amendment, states that early American leaders greatly feared that their democratic system could be abused by corrupt politicians. In the May 1990 issue of *USA Today* magazine, Abrams wrote: "Clearly, in the late 18th century, the framers [of the Second Amendment] feared another all-powerful government like that of the British. . . . Thus, in an effort to protect the

Richard Henry Lee, a signer of the Declaration of Independence, stated that all people should be taught how to use firearms so that they could defend and preserve their liberty.

states from a too-powerful Federal government, the Second Amendment guaranteed states the right to form their own militia to call upon if necessary. Many citizens kept guns in their homes for this purpose."

The young nation could not afford to train and pay a regular standing army, so its leaders made sure that its citizens could be called up to military service at a moment's notice. Keeping guns locked in public arsenals was thought to be impractical and time-consuming. It was better, the leaders argued, to allow citizens the right to keep their weapons at home. If an invading army attempted to conquer the nation, these citizen soldiers could rise in no time to its defense. If the government became corrupt and attempted to subvert democracy, citizens could take up arms and fight to keep the freedoms they had worked so hard to win. This, many historians argue today, was the cornerstone of the right to keep and bear arms. As Richard Henry Lee, a signer of the Declaration of Independence, wrote, "To preserve liberty, it is essential that the whole body of the people always possess arms, and be taught alike, especially the young, how to use them."

A safeguard against tyranny?

As unlikely as it seems today, many people still believe that a tyrannical leader or hostile foreign power could try to take over the United States. The best defense against such a takeover and the loss of individual liberties, some argue, remains an armed citizenry. The late U.S. vice president and Minnesota senator Hubert H. Humphrey said, "The right of citizens to bear arms is just one more guarantee against arbitrary government, one more safeguard against a tyranny which now appears remote in America, but which historically has proved to be always possible." This is one reason activists who favor the right to own guns refuse to support any type of gun control. They fear that gun control laws will become progressively tighter until individuals are no longer allowed to own any type of gun. If that should happen, gun rights groups claim, then the United States would be vulnerable to foreign attack or to a corrupt government that could enforce its rule with little opposition.

But others say that the United States' military forces are enough to defend the country against aggression. Armed citizen soldiers, they maintain, are no longer needed. The time when a farmer or storekeeper grabbed a gun from the mantel and rushed off to war has long since passed. The combined armed forces—Army, Navy, Air Force, Marines, and the National Guard—consist of citizens from all walks of life, and together they serve as the best safeguard against foreign aggression, these people say.

A letter writer to the *New Republic* described the situation this way: "In Thomas Jefferson's day the right to own weapons was the last guarantee against tyranny. In an established democracy, however . . . if all other safeguards against oppression fail, a Saturday Night Special on the nightstand won't make much difference."

Protecting home and family

Some people interpret the Second Amendment as supporting private gun ownership as a means of protecting oneself and one's home and family. For this support, they look to the phrase "security of a free state." This phrase, found in the Second Amendment, has been interpreted by some to mean that citizens have a constitutional right to live without fear in their own homes. This security can be achieved by any lawful means, including owning guns, according to this interpretation.

American soldiers train in the use of firearms. Many people believe that the original intent of the Second Amendment was to provide for the national defense in the absence of a standing army. These people argue that the existence of the U.S. armed forces makes private gun ownership unnecessary today.

Guns were intended to be a "means by which citizens could assure themselves of a right of security," writes Donald L. Bueschle, an assistant professor of law at the John Marshall Law School in Chicago. The NRA echoes this sentiment when it says: "Protection of self, of one's loved ones, of one's home and community is the root of the American tradition of gun ownership."

Is privacy an issue?

The third constitutional issue concerning gun control is the right to privacy. Many people believe that buying a gun is a private decision and that the government has no business gathering information on people who wish to do so. They contend that government involvement in this area is an intrusion into a person's private life. Lawyer Stephen P. Halbrook argues that the right to own a gun is as important as the constitutional right to free speech. He believes free speech and the right to bear arms were equally well laid out by the nation's founders. According to Halbrook, both are guaranteed freedoms. He considers measures like gun registration unconstitutional. Halbrook writes, "No one would seriously argue that citizens must register with the police or obtain a license in order to exercise freely their political or religious beliefs. Requiring citizens to register or obtain a [gun] permit . . . would clearly infringe their rights."

Others, however, do not view gun control measures such as registration as violating a person's privacy. Even in a free society, they contend, privacy has its limits. In order to assure public safety or collect taxes, for example, the government sometimes requires certain information from citizens. In many cases, requiring citizens to register certain items and provide personal information is not considered burdensome. For example, most people accept that cars and motorcycles must be registered and licensed. Most people accept that registration, in this case, is for the public good. Gun registration advocates maintain that firearms should be treated no differently.

Pete Shields, the chairman of HCI, argues that one's privacy is invaded almost daily in more disturbing ways. For example, he writes, "The average citizen is subjected to credit verification

© Ross/Rothco. Reprinted by permission.

ROTHCO

"WELL, WELL, THE RIGHT TO BEAR ARMS"

when buying something with a credit card; only when the clerk has made sure your name is not on a list of known deadbeats will he or she approve your purchase. Does the NRA think this is an unfair infringement of the freedom of law-abiding citizens?" Shields rejects the argument that gun controls such as registration would violate a person's privacy. He believes the public benefit of requiring registration outweighs the small loss of privacy.

Others contend that the Second Amendment has nothing to do with individual citizens and privacy. It says nothing about individuals taking up arms for their own sake, these people say. The Second Amendment talks only of the protection of the country by the people as a whole, as a collective unit, and this purpose is served by the nation's police and armed forces. In *The Right to Bear Arms*, Carl Bakal argues that the Second Amendment "refers only to the people's collective right to bear arms as members of a well-regulated and authorized militia." The Constitution does not guarantee private citizens a right to own guns, Bakal says. It only allows them to own firearms if they serve as part of a defending national army.

Understanding the Second Amendment today

With conflicting notions of what the Second Amendment means, disputes over how it should be applied today occur frequently. As with many other disagreements over interpretation of laws, disputes over whether gun control is constitutional periodically end up in the courts. In these cases, the courts are asked to interpret the Constitution as it applies to modern-day situations.

On the subject of gun control, the courts have mostly been asked to determine the amount of control federal, state, and local governments may

This Morton Grove, Illinois, sporting goods shop owner closed out his entire inventory of guns when sales dropped after the city passed a strict gun control ordinance in 1981.

have over private ownership of firearms. In 1939, for instance, the United States Supreme Court banned most sawed-off shotguns from private ownership. The court ruled that this firearm, which was often used to commit crime, had little use in providing national security, therefore it was not protected by the Second Amendment.

More recent decisions in the courts have also upheld various gun control laws. One such case involved the city of Chicago and a man named Jerome Sklar. Sklar moved to Chicago in 1982 from the nearby suburb of Skokie. Among Sklar's belongings was a handgun, which he had bought legally in Skokie. As it happened, just one month before Sklar moved, a new law went into effect in Chicago. This law required handgun owners to register their guns with the city by April 10. All handguns not registered by that date would be considered illegal and subject to confiscation by police. Since Sklar moved to Chicago on April 15, five days after the registration deadline, he was not allowed to legally bring his handgun to Chicago.

Sklar thought Chicago's ordinance violated his constitutional right to keep and bear arms, so he challenged the law in court. City officials had not concerned themselves with constitutional issues. They had only wanted to restrict handgun ownership in hopes of seeing a reduction in gun violence in their city. Sklar's case went through the courts until it reached the federal court of appeals. The appellate judges ruled in 1984 that the Chicago City Council had not violated any constitutional principles and had acted "to protect the health and safety of its citizens."

A fundamental right?

The ruling was important because it reinforced the idea that government has a right to limit the types of weapons private citizens can own. In so ruling, the court expressed its belief that gun ownership is not an absolute constitutional right. The authors of *Gun Control: Protecting Rights or Protecting People?* write that the courts "did not see the possession of a handgun as a fundamental right protected by either the federal or state constitution."

The 1981 handgun ban in Morton Grove, Illinois, has also been challenged in the courts. Seven Morton Grove residents, backed by the NRA, filed a lawsuit in 1983 claiming that the ban violated their constitutional rights. Like the federal Constitution, the Illinois Constitution refers to a citizen's right to bear arms. It states that "subject only to the police power, the right to bear arms shall not be infringed." Morton Grove officials countered that local police had the power to ban certain weapons that posed a threat to the "peace and stability" of the community. They also claimed that the Illinois Constitution only guaranteed the right to own some guns. Their ordinance, they stated, simply banned handguns, not all guns, so the residents of Morton Grove could still possess guns for hunting, for example. City officials also argued that sufficient legal precedence for gun control measures existed to uphold their law. The courts agreed. In all, the case was heard by four lower courts that ruled that the ordinance was not unconstitutional. Finally, the Illinois Supreme Court decided that "the ordinance is a proper exercise of the police power." The Morton Grove handgun ban still stands.

Despite the court rulings which generally favor certain controls, the issue has not been settled. Cases involving new gun laws constantly crop up, calling for additional interpretations by the courts. Other cases will almost certainly come before U.S. courts, once again testing the constitutional limits of gun control. But for now, these cases offer a guide as to the constitutionality of some gun control measures.

4

Can Gun Control Reduce Crime?

VIOLENT CRIME is the number one concern of millions of Americans. According to a 1989 poll published in *Parents* magazine, 82 percent of American adults believe crime is a serious problem. And according to a 1991 *U.S. News & World Report* survey, 60 percent are afraid of being attacked in their homes. Urban residents, the survey showed, especially fear attackers armed with guns. The FBI's 1990 crime statistics indicate that guns are often used in crime. FBI director William Sessions reported that in 1990, 23,438 people were murdered in the United States. Three out of every five of those victims were shot to death. Another 236,530 people were robbed at gunpoint during the same year.

Searching for answers

Politicians and law-enforcement officials have long sought methods to curb gun-related crime. Some say the amount of violence in American society is directly related to the number of guns in public hands. Gun control is favored by many as a crucial step toward a solution. But Americans are divided over whether gun control would actually reduce crime.

(opposite page) A man uses an illegal sawed-off shotgun to rob a bank as a customer lies face down on the floor. Gun control advocates and critics debate whether gun control can reduce crime.

Those who support bans, for example, say they offer one quick way to reduce gun violence in the United States. Law professors Franklin E. Zimring and Gordon Hawkins write that "substantially reducing the number of handguns should reduce the number of homicides resulting from accidental weapon use and the use of a weapon to settle an argument."

Those who oppose gun bans say bans have little effect on crime and that they penalize gun collectors and others who may have a legitimate reason to own guns. These people say that bans do not reduce crime. Don Feder, a Boston *Herald* columnist, writes, "Boston banned semi-automatic weapons in 1990. . . . Washington has

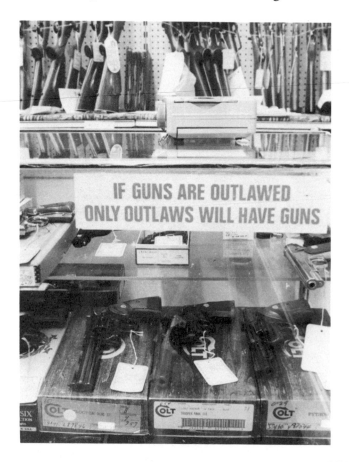

An antigun control slogan displayed in a gun shop implies that unarmed law-abiding citizens will be at the mercy of armed criminals if guns are outlawed.

banned the sale of handguns and outlawed ownership of any handguns not licensed prior to 1977. Each city posted a record number of homicides in 1990."

A mixed bag of results

The Massachusetts Bartley-Fox law is often cited as an example of a gun control measure that has successfully reduced crime. The 1974 law requires a mandatory jail sentence for carrying a handgun outside one's home or place of business without a permit. According to a Northeastern University study, Boston's handgun murder rate dropped 50 percent and the armed robbery rate dropped 35 percent after the law was enacted.

New Jersey's background checks and thirty-day waiting period for handgun buyers have been cited as another success. According to one gun control supporter, more than ten thousand felons have been prevented from getting handguns since the checks began in 1970.

However, figures in other cities and states cast some doubt on gun control's ability to reduce crime. A study of Detroit's gun laws, published in the May 1991 issue of the *American Journal of Public Health*, found that gun crime actually increased after a new gun control measure took effect. An ordinance, which became effective on January 10, 1987, imposed a mandatory prison sentence for anyone caught unlawfully carrying a gun in public. The ordinance had been passed in response to Detroit's high murder rate. According to statistics compiled for the previous fifteen years, Detroit had led the nation in per capita murders twelve out of fifteen years. City council members hoped the mandatory jail sentence would reduce gun crime. The first year the law was in effect, Detroit experienced a 22 percent rise in gun-related murders occurring in homes, public buildings, and bars. Detroit also experienced a 10 percent rise in gun-related murders occurring on streets, in alleyways, or in outdoor public places.

The researchers concluded that no definitive statement could be made about the law's effectiveness. They added that the law was poorly enforced, probably because Detroit's jails were so overcrowded that police hesitated to add to the jail population by arresting people who violated the new law.

Will criminals comply?

The problem with most gun control measures, opponents say, is that gun violence relates not to the number of guns, but to who owns them. A person who is willing to commit a crime is not likely to abide by gun registration laws or even bans, these people say. James D. Wright, a professor of sociology at the University of Massachusetts-Amherst, asks, "Why should we expect felons to comply with a gun law when they readily violate laws against robbery, assault, and murder?"

For this reason, many people argue, restrictive laws will not reduce crime because criminals will still have guns. And if criminals still have guns, violence will continue. New York City, for example, has very tight handgun restrictions. To buy a handgun, city residents must apply to the police for a permit. Very few permits are given out. They go primarily to active-duty and retired police officers, security guards and bodyguards, and prominent people who demonstrate a need to have a gun for protection. In addition, anyone caught carrying a concealed handgun without a permit faces a felony charge and a mandatory prison sentence. Because of these restrictions, as of April 1991 there were only 61,497 legally

Cullum/Copley News Service. Reprinted with permission.

"WE'LL HIT THE LIQUOR STORE ON 48TH....THEN SHOOT UP THE QUIK MART BY THE INTERSTATE... THEN MAYBE LOOK FOR A FEW HOSTAGES... FIRST, THOUGH, WE'LL HAVE TO STOP BY A LICENSED GUN DEALER AND REGISTER OUR FIREARMS."

owned handguns in New York City, a city of seven million people. Yet research indicates that there are at least 750,000 handguns in the city and gun-related crime remains high. In 1989, 70 percent of the city's twenty-two hundred homicides were caused by gunfire. The BATF says that 96 percent of all handguns used for criminal purposes come from outside the city. This means that criminals still obtain handguns for illicit purposes despite New York's tough laws.

Washington, D.C., instituted a handgun ban similar to New York's in 1977. The district's law allows only police officers and security guards to purchase or carry handguns. The experience of Washington, D.C., has mirrored New York's. The murder rate remains high. According to 1988 FBI statistics, Washington led the nation with a murder rate of 59.5 deaths per 100,000 residents. Even Washington police chief Maurice Turner viewed the ban as completely ineffective. "What has the gun control law done to keep criminals from getting guns? Absolutely nothing," Turner said. Violent crime is so common in Washington, D.C., that Turner even suggested that district residents should buy handguns for protection. "[City residents] ought to have the opportunity to have a handgun," Turner said.

Guns at home

If a gun in the home offers personal protection, it might also serve as a deterrent to neighborhood crime, some people think. The National Institute of Justice, a research organization based in Wash-

Don Eckelkamp. The New American. Printed with permission.

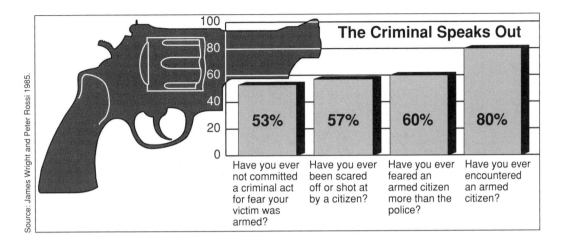

Source: James Wright and Peter Rossi 1985.

The Criminal Speaks Out

| 53% | 57% | 60% | 80% |

Have you ever not committed a criminal act for fear your victim was armed?

Have you ever been scared off or shot at by a citizen?

Have you ever feared an armed citizen more than the police?

Have you ever encountered an armed citizen?

ington, D.C., tried to find out if this was the case.

The institute surveyed eighteen hundred prison inmates nationwide in a study done in the early 1980s. Among other questions, researchers asked inmates if they carried out a crime once they discovered the potential victim had a gun. Forty percent of the inmates taking part in the survey said they broke off their attacks when they realized their intended targets had guns. This study has been cited as evidence that guns in the home or place of business deter and thus reduce crime.

There have been times when a gun in the home did, in fact, help stop a crime. The NRA has collected many such stories. In one pamphlet, the organization tells the story of a Waco, Texas homemaker who heard someone breaking into her house shortly after her husband left for work. She ran to her bedroom, locked the door, and grabbed a handgun hidden beneath the mattress. The intruder followed her to the bedroom and kicked open the door. When he saw the gun, he turned and fled.

But others say these cases are few. Instead, they say that guns kept for protection and deterrence are more often used accidentally against friends and family or in suicides. In *Gun Control:*

A Decision for Americans, Edward F. Dolan Jr., cites a study conducted over a twenty-year period by Norman Rushforth at Case Western Reserve University. The study, completed in the 1970s, showed that guns kept for protection are six times more likely to be used—either accidentally or on purpose—for killing family members and friends than for shooting unknown attackers. The researchers also stated that 70 percent of handgun shootings occurred between relatives or acquaintances. Instead of providing protection and deterring crime, guns kept in the home actually added to the danger, Dolan concluded based on this study.

Guns intended for protection and deterrence also play a key role in suicides. According to 1987 statistics from the U.S. Bureau of the Census, 64 percent of men who commit suicide do it with a gun. For women, the rate is 41 percent. Michael K. Beard, the executive director of the National Coalition to Ban Handguns, writes, "Twelve thousand people commit suicide with handguns each year. Mental health professionals agree that up to 60 percent of handgun suicides would not have occurred were it not for the immediate presence of a lethal weapon."

Reducing accidents

Likewise, handguns kept in homes are often mistakenly used as playthings by children who do not realize their danger. In 1988, 1,501 Americans died in accidental shootings. While over half of these were hunting mishaps, hundreds involved children accidentally shooting each other with their parents' guns. Gun control advocates believe that stricter measures will reduce the number of guns in private hands, thereby reducing the chance of such accidents occurring.

Many stories of tragic accidents involving chil-

A woman loads her .357 Magnum for target practice at a shooting range. Opponents of gun control contend that proper training in handling guns prevents accidents.

dren and guns have been told. HCI has collected many such accounts. In one publication the organization tells the story of a Pottstown, Pennsylvania man who bought a .22 caliber pistol to protect his family after burglars had robbed his home three times in two weeks. He practiced shooting the gun and then set it down with the ammunition clip removed. The man's 5-year-old son picked the gun up to play with it. One bullet remained in the chamber. The boy examined the small, toylike gun, pulled the trigger, and accidentally shot himself to death. The father advised gun owners, "All I can say to anyone who has a handgun in the house is get rid of it. It's not worth it."

Opponents of gun control say that these cases are the exception. In many households where guns are present, the adult owners use and store them wisely and cautiously and often teach chil-

© Dick Adair/Rothco. Reprinted by permission.

dren proper handling techniques. Though tragic, accidental gun deaths like the one that occurred in Pottstown do not happen as frequently as other accidents leading to death. Alan Gottlieb maintains that a person is twenty-six times more likely to die in a car accident than to be killed accidentally by a gun. And yet the government does not try to ban cars. Instead, authorities try to better educate the public to proper uses of cars. This, too, should be the response to guns, some gun control opponents contend.

The difficulties of enforcement

There is one point in the debate over gun control on which many people agree—although perhaps for different reasons. Many people believe that one of the greatest obstacles to gun control reducing crime is that many measures are difficult to enforce. In many cases, gun owners simply ignore them. If gun control measures cannot be enforced, most people agree, they cannot reduce crime.

For example, owners of semiautomatic rifles largely ignored the 1990 California law requiring them to register their weapons. The law stated that all semiautomatic rifles purchased before June 1989 had to be registered by January 1, 1990, or they would be considered illegal and could be confiscated. However, by the time the deadline passed, only 42,809 of the estimated 300,000 rifles had been registered. Unless California police officials conduct house-to-house searches, which is highly impractical and unlikely, most assault rifles will never be registered or seized. The lack of public cooperation causes most gun control analysts to conclude that such measures will not reduce crime.

Proponents of gun control as a crime-reducing measure suggest that enforcement of consistent, national laws would not be difficult. What makes gun control ineffective in cutting crime now, they argue, is the number of differing local and state laws. With more than twenty thousand gun control measures in fifty states, enforcement and effectiveness are a problem. If states had uniform laws, gun control supporters believe, criminals would be frustrated in their attempts to get guns, thus reducing the crime rate. Pete Shields writes, "Across America, cities are trying to do something about the handgun problem. But too often their efforts are hampered by . . . weak or nonexistent laws in neighboring states. The national situation calls out for a federal handgun control law."

Not everyone agrees with this position. Some people argue that gun control of any kind only superficially addresses the nation's crime problems. Instead, the nation's leaders need to deal with the underlying causes of crime, such as poverty, unemployment, and hopelessness. Only then, they argue, will crime in the United States decrease.

Maida Vale Edgware Rd
Oxford Street Holborn
St.Pauls Liverpool St
ST. PAULS
British Museum & The City
LITTLEWOODS
RM1303
303 CLT

5

Guns and Gun Control in Other Countries

UNLIKE THE UNITED STATES, many industrialized nations strictly limit or ban private gun ownership. Some of these countries have long histories of limits on gun ownership. Yet gun control has never sparked the controversy elsewhere that it has in this nation. In contrast to the American experience, gun control in other countries has generally been a quiet process involving little debate or public outcry.

The reasons for this could be many. Americans relied on guns to help settle the country. They used guns to fight off British rule and to establish a new country. They created a unique Constitution that guaranteed certain individual liberties, including the right to an armed citizen militia. And they have maintained ties to guns through hobbies and sports such as target shooting, gun collecting, and hunting. Americans' strong historical ties to guns have made gun control an emotional issue.

For this reason, some Americans have looked outside their own country for guidance and ideas.

(opposite page) English police officers, or bobbies, were traditionally unarmed. Gun control has not been a big issue in Great Britain where comparatively few citizens own guns.

65

The experiences of other nations may prove useful to Americans who continue to wrestle with this difficult issue.

The Japanese experience

One nation with a long history of gun control is Japan. Japan's gun control laws are considered among the toughest in the world. But guns have never really played a large part in Japan's history, culture, or recreation. Though the Japanese were early experts with gunpowder, they chose not to develop guns for nearly two hundred years. Instead, they turned to the sword as their instrument of battle.

Firearms first came to Japan in 1543 with the arrival of European traders. The Japanese gun-making industry soon blossomed and guns became a common weapon of warfare for the next sixty years. However, at the beginning of the seventeenth century, shogun leaders rose to power and began to discourage the use of guns. Under the shogun leadership a class of professional warriors, called samurai, prospered. Like their military leaders, the samurai disdained guns for their noise and lack of grace. Instead, they found honor in fighting their battles with swords. Samurai warriors viewed the use of a musket to kill enemy warriors a disgrace. They preferred the grace and athleticism of prolonged hand-to-hand sword fights. Like the six-shooter in the American West, the sword became a symbol of Japanese culture. "The sword was not merely a fighting weapon in Japan," writes Noel Perrin in his book *Giving Up the Gun*, "it was the visible form of one's honour—'the soul of the samurai.'"

For two centuries, from the 1650s to the 1850s, guns were largely ignored as fighting weapons in Japan. Only with the arrival of Commodore Matthew Perry's fleet from the United States in

1854 were guns reintroduced to the culture. Even then, samurai warriors resisted using them. When the last of the shogun leaders fell from power in the 1870s, new Japanese leaders banned the wearing of swords. For the samurai this was a sign that Western culture was taking over their way of life. In 1877 they rebelled. They went to battle wearing their traditional kimonos and carrying only their swords against armed government troops. Their rebellion was quickly crushed and the era of the Japanese sword effectively ended.

From then on Japanese leaders encouraged gun making for military purposes. By the late 1930s the government had amassed an arsenal of mil-

Japanese samurai warriors preferred swords to guns in battle. The honor-bound samurai deemed guns crude and disgraceful to use against enemies. The sword, therefore, not the gun, became a symbol of power and honor in Japan.

Although these World War II Japanese soldiers use firearms, they also carry swords as a mark of tradition and honor. Confident of victory, most exultantly raise their swords rather than their guns.

lions of weapons. But in contrast to the American experience, these guns were not for civilian use. At the end of World War II, surplus military guns were not allowed to fall into civilian hands. After Japan lost the war, gun restrictions were instituted by the victorious Allied military commanders who ran Japan. From 1945 to 1950 the private ownership of guns and swords was banned. The Allied commanders wanted to ensure that Japanese society became completely demilitarized. In 1950, when Japanese leaders again assumed power, gun control measures were kept largely intact. Little protest was heard because, for the most part, Japanese citizens had never become used to the personal right to own guns.

That trend continues today in Japan, where few citizens own guns. Those that are privately owned are strictly controlled. In a country of 120 million people, there are only 27,000 licensed rifles and 500,000 licensed shotguns. These guns are used primarily for hunting or competitive target shooting. Licenses for these weapons can only be obtained after taking a gun safety course and obtaining permission from a public safety commission. Private citizens may not own handguns of any kind. Only public officials such as police officers and prison guards are granted permits to own handguns.

Some people attribute Japan's exceptionally low gun-related crime rate to its strict gun control laws. According to the World Health Organization, 112 Japanese citizens died from gunshot wounds in 1987. Though it has half the population of the United States, Japan's handgun murder rate is two hundred times lower than that in the United States and its armed robbery rate is one hundred times lower. Many American gun control activists would like to see Japanese-style gun control laws implemented in this country.

Others, however, attribute Japan's low crime rate to other factors. Many analysts believe that gun control laws should not be given credit for Japan's low rate of violent crime. Instead, they maintain, credit should go to Japan's law-enforcement agencies and strict court system. According to David Hardy of the scholarly magazine *Reason*, Japanese authorities solve 81 percent of their violent crimes, while the United States solves only 45 percent. That, they claim, is the true reason for Japan's low gun crime rate.

Whatever the reasons for these low gun crime figures, few analysts believe Japan's strict gun controls would be accepted in the United States. For this reason, many gun control advocates look to other nations for models.

The British experience

Great Britain is one. The nation from which the United States sprang has a long history of gun control. Yet this tradition did not carry over to the

United States when it broke from Britain's grasp. While Americans came to value their firearms highly, guns have never played a large role in daily British life or culture. This stems from the fact that guns in Britain were largely tools of the military and the privileged nobility. To maintain power, many English monarchs of the seventeenth and eighteenth centuries restricted access to guns. They did not want common people to own guns. Leaders like King George I feared that popular, armed rebellions might one day sweep them from power. Shortly after he became king, George I ordered his officials in Scotland "to search for and seize all arms, ammunition, and other warlike stores."

So, unlike the Americans who relied on citizen soldiers for national defense, the British relied on armies led by the nobility. By putting the rich and powerful in charge of the army, British monarchs ensured that those who controlled the weapons had a stake in preserving the ruling system. This exclusive system effectively kept firearms out of the hands of ordinary men and women.

Lack of popular interest for guns

Likewise, hunting was viewed as a sport for the upper class. This arose from two factors. One, early muskets were complicated, expensive items that most people could not afford. The second factor was that to hunt in Britain one needed to own land or know someone who owned land because there were no public hunting grounds. Since only a tiny percentage of the population were landowners, few British citizens had the right to hunt. As a result, most British subjects had little or no experience with guns. Even after the development of cheaper weapons, no strong gun tradition developed in Britain. Since few people cared about gun ownership, little protest was

Eighteenth-century British king George I disarmed the common people of his realm to prevent rebellion.

raised when gun control laws came into being.

Britain's first modern comprehensive gun control act was passed in 1920. Spurred by the availability of guns after World War I, the Firearms Act required that all buyers of weapons other than shotguns get a certificate from the local police. The certificates were issued only if the police felt the buyer posed no dire threat to public safety. Little discussion surrounded this measure. In the 1960s additional laws were passed limiting private citizens' rights to own handguns and requiring a certificate for shotgun owners.

Besides limiting private ownership of guns, Britain also preserves a largely unarmed police force, casually called bobbies. Most British bobbies do not carry guns. The notion of an unarmed police force astounds most Americans, but to the British it is familiar. Even today few British citi-

An engraving portrays two English noblemen hunting pheasant. Historically, the ruling nobility and royalty were the only Britons who owned guns.

A typical English bobby walks his beat armed with only a whistle.

zens own guns and Britain has relatively few gun crimes.

Despite increases in violent crime in recent years, Britain's gun crime rate remains low. In 1988, thirty-six people were killed by firearms in Britain. During the same year, ten thousand people were killed by guns in the United States.

These types of figures did not offer much comfort to British citizens, who demanded even stronger laws in the late 1980s. These demands came in the wake of a killing spree by Michael Ryan in the English town of Hungerford on August 19, 1987. Ryan, armed with an AK-47 assault rifle and two pistols, all of which he had purchased legally, calmly walked through Hungerford and killed fifteen people before killing himself. Ryan's murderous assault shocked the nation and prompted demands for stronger gun control.

Strict laws get even tougher

In response to public outcry over the Hungerford killings, British lawmakers tightened gun restrictions. They sought to eliminate from general circulation rapid-firing and easily concealed firearms as well as those that are lethal over a wide area at short range. Toward this end, British lawmakers passed a 1988 law banning all semi-automatic rifles larger than .22 caliber, all pump-action rifles, and all shotguns with barrels shorter than twenty-four inches. In banning these weapons, British lawmakers hoped to prevent further tragedies like the Hungerford rampage.

Many analysts believe that Britain's gun control measures could work in the United States. Britain, like the United States, is facing a growing violent crime problem. Drug gangs are turning to firearms for protection, and physical assault is on the rise. Despite this, gun control supporters claim, Britain's gun controls keep violent gun-related crime in check.

Writers for the conservative magazine *The American Spectator* concur that the low murder rate in Britain stems from that nation's tough gun laws. "Firearm laws in Britain are strict," they write. "Britain, whose population is nearly one hundred times Washington's, has fewer than twice the number of murders, despite a slowly but steadily worsening drug problem." The United States, they suggest, should adopt some of Britain's tough gun control measures.

Other gun control analysts counter that Britain had fewer murders than the United States even before its gun control laws went into effect. This means factors other than gun control may be responsible for Britain's low crime rate. "In the 1920s, before Britain had its restrictive gun laws, the British murder rate was still less than in the United States. Obviously, then, the difference in homicide rates is due to something more than just gun control," Alan Gottlieb writes. If this is the case, people like Gottlieb argue, then transplanting Britain's laws to the United States would not reduce gun-related crime.

The Canadian experience

Though British law and history have had a strong influence on the United States, some gun control advocates believe Canada offers the best model for effective gun laws. According to Canada's Justice Department, 23 percent of the nation's households own firearms. The country's 25 million citizens own 5.9 million guns. Gun control supporters say that despite the large number of guns, Canada has a surprisingly low gun crime rate. In 1989, only 219 Canadians were murdered by guns. In the United States, which has ten times more people than Canada, the gun death rate is about seventy times higher. According to U.S. government statistics, about fourteen thousand Americans were shot to death in 1990.

Canada has enforced handgun restrictions for more than a century. An 1877 law mandated penalties for those who carried handguns without a reasonable need for self-defense. In 1934, the Canadian parliament passed legislation requiring handgun registration.

Canada's modern federal gun law was enacted in 1977. This law required citizens to obtain certificates from local police before buying shotguns and rifles. People under the age of sixteen or those who had been convicted of a criminal offense, treated as a mental patient within the previous five years, or had acted or threatened to act violently within the previous five years, were prohibited from obtaining a certificate.

The 1977 law also placed additional restrictions on handguns. To obtain a handgun permit,

This early photograph shows a Canadian mounted policeman aiming a rifle. Canadians traditionally have preferred rifles to handguns. Some people say this tradition, plus strict handgun laws, keeps handgun-related crime low in Canada.

individuals must explain to police why they need a handgun. For example, the applicant must show cause that the gun is needed for personal protection, protection of business interests, for work as a security guard or bodyguard, as part of a gun collection, or for target practice at an established shooting club. These restrictions, along with Canadians' traditional preference for long guns such as rifles over other firearms, have kept the number of handguns in private possession relatively low. Of the five million guns owned by Canadians, only 300,000 are handguns. And of the more than two hundred annual gun deaths in Canada, only a quarter are attributed to handguns.

Responding to tragedy

But recent events have caused many Canadians to argue that even these gun restrictions are not enough. On a dark December evening in 1989, gun enthusiast Marc Lepine burst into a classroom at Montreal's Ecole Polytechnique University and ordered all the women students to stand in a line. Armed with a semiautomatic Ruger Mini-14 rifle, Lepine then started shooting the women. Fourteen died. In all, Lepine shot twenty-seven people before turning the gun on himself. The Canadian public was shocked and outraged by Lepine's actions. Many demanded new, stronger gun control laws.

Among the proposals introduced after the Montreal tragedy were bills calling for a twenty-eight-day waiting period and the submission of photo identification and two character references when applying for firearm certificates. During the waiting period, local police would be responsible for conducting thorough background checks on all applicants.

The photo identification would assure police that the applicant is actually the person attempt-

Canadian mass murderer Marc Lepine legally bought a semiautomatic rifle and killed fourteen university students in Montreal in 1989. Canadians urged stricter gun control laws after Lepine's spree.

ing to buy the gun and is not buying it for someone else. The character references would put friends or associates on record as verifying the sanity of the applicant. The bill's supporters say they believe few people would vouch for others they do not think are fit to handle a gun responsibly. Lepine bought his gun legally, according to Canada's existing laws. The bill's supporters hope that these additional requirements, especially character references, would keep someone like Lepine from buying a gun in the future. Canadian legislators hope to complete debate on these proposed laws by 1992.

Canadian lawmakers have also proposed limits on rifle clip sizes. Lepine's Ruger had a thirty-shot clip, meaning he did not have to stop and reload until all thirty bullets were fired. The proposed legislation calls for a five-bullet limit on clips.

Similarities and differences

Gun control advocates in the United States view Canada's laws as perhaps the best model for the United States. They cite the similarities be-

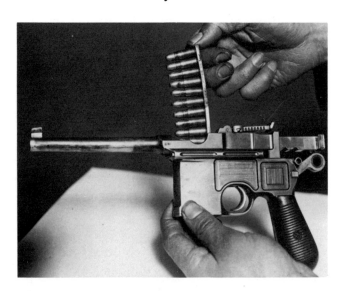

A gun clip holds multiple rounds that can be fired in rapid succession before reloading. Some gun control advocates want the number of rounds in a clip to be limited.

Pioneers in both the United States and Canada armed themselves with guns for survival. The Canadian pioneering experience, however, did not generate a dependency on firearms the way it did in the United States.

tween the two countries as other reasons for following Canada's lead. Both countries were settled by immigrants and rapidly expanded westward. Both encountered a native Indian population in the drive west and relied on guns to survive in the rugged wilderness. In addition, in both countries, the pioneer heritage and vast wildlife areas have made hunting a popular national pastime.

But Canada and the United States also differ in many ways, including in history, wartime experience, and population. For these and other reasons, Canadians never seemed to develop a dependence on guns the way Americans did.

William R. Tonso, an associate professor of sociology at the University of Evansville in Indiana, argues that the differences in the two countries' attitudes toward guns stem from differing pioneering pasts. For this reason, he does not believe Canadian gun control measures would work well in the United States. Relations between Canadian settlers and native Indians were not nearly as hostile as those that developed in the United States, for example. Other than for hunting, Tonso believes, Canadians did not develop the same psychological reliance on guns as Americans did.

Tonso also writes that Canada's frontier police forces had more success in maintaining law and order than did their American counterparts. For this reason, Canadian settlers rarely had to enforce the law themselves. Gun-wielding rustlers and outlaws were not the threat in the young Canada that they were in the young United States.

In addition, Canada has never fought a bloody revolutionary war or a divisive civil war where nearly every citizen took up arms. Unlike the United States, Canada's independence from Britain came through peaceful means. Hence, Canadians have less reason to view guns as the preserving force of freedom. They did not violently overthrow an oppressive government or experience the flood of firearms a national war brings. And, most telling, Canadians have no constitutional guarantee of a right to bear arms.

Population is one other factor often cited to ex-

Mike Peters. Reprinted with permission.

plain the difference in gun violence between the countries. The United States has ten times the population that Canada has. While the United States has dozens of large, poor, overcrowded urban centers where crime is prevalent, Canada only has a handful. Enforcing stringent gun control measures in a country the size of the United States would be extremely difficult, many observers say. The Canadians succeed, they suggest, because their task of controlling guns involves smaller cities and fewer people.

Balancing rights and needs

Many nations seem to have succeeded in reducing gun crimes through strict gun control laws. But opinions differ on whether any of these laws can be transplanted to the United States. David B. Kopel, an attorney and writer for the NRA's monthly magazine, *American Rifleman*, echoes a popular sentiment when he writes, "The gun controls that other nations have chosen for themselves simply would not work in the United States."

However, many gun control advocates believe that Americans can learn from the experience of other nations. Ultimately, though, Americans must create their own solutions to a unique problem, balancing the rights of the gun-owning public with the effort to reduce violent crime.

Epilogue

THE LANDSCAPE of gun control legislation is constantly evolving as states add and delete laws in hopes of curing the rising crime problem. Popular opinion, however, seems to be shifting more strongly in favor of increased gun control measures. According to a Gallup poll taken in March 1991, 87 percent of Americans favor a seven-day waiting period for handgun buyers.

The Brady Bill

A federal seven-day waiting period for any handgun purchase is the core of a bill that was under discussion in 1991. This bill is known as the Brady Bill. Although this bill would not require background checks of potential buyers, it is believed that most states would use the time to examine the buyer's records for evidence of mental illness or criminal activity. Though the bill seems relatively weak compared to various state gun control measures, the Brady Bill is significant because it would be the first tightening of federal gun control law since 1968.

After a fierce, much-publicized debate, the U.S. House of Representatives passed the Brady Bill in May 1991. Soon after that, the Senate adopted a comprehensive crime bill that includes a five-day waiting period for handgun purchases. A national computer system would even-

(opposite page) Shooting enthusiasts use high-tech sighting equipment to improve their accuracy at long range. Future gun control legislation may limit the use of sophisticated firearms to shooting ranges like this one.

James Brady gives the victory sign following the passage of the House's Brady Bill, which would require a seven-day waiting period on handgun purchases.

tually replace the five-day waiting period with instant background checks, according to the Senate bill. The House and Senate were expected to discuss a compromise that would go before President George Bush for signature.

Brady Bill supporters hope the law will save lives by denying handguns to criminals, drug dealers, and the mentally ill. By instituting a uniform national waiting period, the bill's backers say, convicted felons will not be able to legally purchase handguns in states with lax laws. Many police officials support the bill, saying it will help reduce street crime. Houston police captain Bill Edison says, "I can't sit out here amongst the carnage I see on the streets and not support a waiting bill. A waiting period will save x number of lives. How many, we could argue about forever."

The Brady Bill is named after James Brady, who served as former president Reagan's press secretary. Brady was shot in the head during John Hinckley's 1981 assassination attempt on Reagan. Brady recovered from the shooting but still suffers from painful headaches and slurred speech, and must rely on a wheelchair and cane to move around. Brady and his wife, Sarah Brady, began speaking out for national handgun restrictions after the attack. In the shooting, Hinckley used a Saturday Night Special that he had legally purchased for twenty-nine dollars. The Bradys believe a seven-day waiting period may in the future give police time to stop mentally unbalanced handgun buyers like Hinckley.

Support and opposition

Police officials across the country have also strongly supported the measure. The Law Enforcement Steering Committee, representing more than 400,000 police officers, supports the bill. According to Gerald Williams, president of the Police Executive Research Forum, "Police know a national program would prevent felons from going to states with weak gun laws and bringing weapons back into those with strong laws to commit crimes. . . . Cops know: seven days can save a life."

Many politicians also favor the bill. Former president Reagan, who for years opposed handgun restrictions, publicly voiced his support for the bill in 1991. Representatives and mayors from crime-ridden urban cities especially support the Brady Bill as a way to curb violent crime. New York City mayor David Dinkins calls the bill "a declaration of domestic disarmament."

Not all lawmakers view the bill so favorably, however. Many legislators and law-enforcement officials see it as a burden on their police forces.

Others see it as a nuisance that will do little to keep guns out of criminals' hands. Congressman John Dingell of Michigan believes "The Brady Bill accomplishes nothing." Many argue that the time and money needed to perform background checks will burden their staffs and keep police officers off the streets where they can do more good. In response to such concerns, Congressman Harley Staggers of West Virginia introduced a countermeasure to the Brady Bill. This measure, which was rejected by the House, called for instant background checks in place of a seven-day waiting period.

An alternative to the Brady Bill?

Staggers's bill would have worked much like the background check system in place in Virginia. There, police refer to their computerized criminal

Bob Gorrell. Reprinted with permission.

record system to check on potential handgun owners. Acceptance or rejection of an application to buy a handgun is almost immediate. The system has halted the sale of 1,475 handguns since it took effect on November 1, 1989. The instant background check has received the support of police officers like Sheriff Don Boswell of Virginia's Henrico County because it is "fast, fair, and it works."

Critics of the Staggers bill said it would be impractical on a nationwide scale because of cost and a current lack of centralized federal criminal records. Sarah Brady, who favored the Brady Bill over the Staggers bill, estimated that it would take $70 million to enter all the criminal data into a national computer system, and another $75 million in annual costs to operate it.

Assault rifles raise new concerns

While much of the gun control debate focuses on the Brady Bill and waiting periods, a secondary wave of gun control activism has sought to restrict assault rifles. Increasing use of assault weapons in drug-related violence has heightened public concern. So have deadly rampages like the 1989 Stockton, California, shooting.

Both California and New Jersey enacted strict assault rifle laws in 1989 and 1990, but New Jersey's law was by far the tougher of the two. The New Jersey ban, which went into effect on May 31, 1991, gave assault rifle owners one year to sell their guns out of state, render them inoperable by removing the firing pins, or surrender them to police. While the law has been very unpopular with gun owners, it is extremely well liked by gun control advocates who hope similar laws will spread across the country. An editorial in the *New York Times* says, "New Jersey's law . . . ought to set an example for other states

A fourteen-year-old California boy tries out a .44 Magnum equipped with a telescopic sight at a National Rifle Association convention.

and the Federal Government."

An effort to amend the law, to allow people who owned assault rifles before 1990 to keep their guns, proved unsuccessful. Gun rights activists said the provision was needed in light of the poor response to the assault rifle ban. According to the *New York Times*, as of June 3, 1991, only 191 owners had disabled their assault rifles and just one had turned his gun in to police. This was out of an estimated 100,000 to 200,000 assault rifles in New Jersey. New Jersey governor James Florio rejected these arguments and vetoed the change. So New Jersey's assault rifle ban, the toughest in the nation, stands.

New Jersey's law may well serve as a model for new gun control legislation across the nation.

State, local, and federal politicians constantly search for new methods of fighting violent crime, and public sentiment seems to favor tougher gun control measures. However, legislators must balance their desire to rid criminals of guns with the knowledge that Americans enjoy their right to keep and bear arms. The difficulty of achieving this balance burst vividly into the American consciousness October 16, 1991. On that day, the Texas town of Killeen became the site of the deadliest mass shooting in United States history. Twenty-three died and nearly two dozen others were wounded when a man named George Hennard crashed his truck into a local cafeteria and began shooting.

The following day, the House of Representatives rejected proposed federal bans on various assault weapons and on large-capacity ammunition clips. The guns used by Hennard were not among the thirteen weapons covered by the proposed ban. But the seventeen-round clips used by the gunman would have been prohibited under the ban.

The tragic shooting in Killeen prompted genuine expressions of grief and horror from all corners of the nation. On this, gun control proponents and opponents are not divided. The shooting did not bring agreement, however, on how best to prevent such tragedies. The vote of 247 to 177 once again illustrated the sharp divisions that remain on the issue of gun control.

The gun control debate may see no end anytime soon. The presence of approximately 165 million guns in American hands guarantees that no easy compromises will be reached.

Glossary

AK-47: A Soviet assault rifle that is popular the world over.

automatic weapon: A gun that continues to fire when the trigger is held down; also called a machine gun.

bill: A proposed law that must be approved by legislators, often subject to change before it becomes law.

Bill of Rights: The first ten amendments of the U.S. Constitution.

caliber: The interior diameter of a gun barrel.

constitution: A document created after American independence from Britain that states the basic laws and principles that govern the nation.

handgun: A gun that is small, easily hidden, and can be fired by one hand.

militia: An army of citizens called into action during a time of war.

musket: A gun used during colonial times with a long, smooth barrel; often heavy and inaccurate.

ordinance: A law or regulation passed by a city government.

Pennsylvania rifle: A longer, lighter version of European rifles first made by gunsmiths near Lancaster, Pennsylvania, in the 1720s. Later called the Kentucky rifle after Daniel Boone popularized its use on the Kentucky frontier.

permit: A document needed in some places to buy certain guns; applicant generally must prove to authorities a need for the gun.

registration: The act of recording one's name and gun identification with the local authorities, usually the police.

repeating rifle: A rifle that does not need to be reloaded after each shot.

rifle: A shoulder weapon with spiral grooves cut inside the gun barrel for greater accuracy.

"Saturday Night Special": A small, cheap handgun, usually .32

caliber or less.

Second Amendment: An amendment to the U.S. Constitution adopted in 1789 that states: "A well-regulated militia being necessary to the security of the free State, the right of the people to keep and bear arms shall not be infringed."

semiautomatic weapon: A gun that requires the user to pull the trigger separately for every shot fired.

tyranny: A government in which a single ruler is given absolute power.

Uzi: A small, lightweight automatic gun made in Israel and a favorite weapon of terrorist groups and drug dealers.

Suggestions for Further Reading

Jervis Anderson, *Guns in American Life*. New York: Random House, 1984.

Edward F. Dolan Jr., *Gun Control: A Decision for Americans*. New York: Franklin Watts, 1982.

William Dudley, ed., *Crime and Criminals: Opposing Viewpoints*. San Diego: Greenhaven Press, 1989.

Reuben Greenberg with Arthur Gordon, *Let's Take Back Our Streets*. Chicago: Contemporary Books, 1989.

Janelle Rohr, ed., *Violence in America: Opposing Viewpoints*. San Diego: Greenhaven Press, 1990.

Karen Sagstetter, *Lobbying*. New York: Franklin Watts, 1978.

Geraldine Woods, *The Right to Bear Arms*. New York: Franklin Watts, 1986.

Works Consulted

Daniel Abrams, "The 'Right' to Bear Arms in America," *USA Today,* May 1990.

American Rifleman, "Sheriff Makes the Point: Instant Background Checks Work," May 1991.

Katherine Bishop, "Gun Law's Effectiveness Questioned," *The New York Times,* May 22, 1991.

Joan Biskupic, "Brady's Solid House Victory Is Gun Control Milestone," *Congressional Quarterly Weekly Report,* May 11, 1991.

Sarah Brady, "And the Case Against Them: The Head of Handgun Control Says Weapons Are Killing the Future," *Time,* January 29, 1990.

Thomas Draper, ed., *The Issue of Gun Control.* New York: H.W. Wilson, 1981.

Andrew Erdman, "Inside the U.S. Gun Business," *Fortune,* June 3, 1991.

Don Feder, "Gun Control Doesn't Work," *New Dimensions,* April 1991.

Alan M. Gottlieb, *Gun Rights Fact Book.* Bellevue, WA: Merril Press, 1988.

Daniel Kagan, "New York's Pistol Licensing: Loaded Dice and Blind Alleys," *Insight,* April 15, 1991.

Lee Kennett and James LaVerne Anderson, *The Gun in America.* Westport, CT: Greenwood Press, 1975.

Wayne King, "New Jersey Assault-Weapon Ban Nets One Gun and Many Appeals," *The New York Times,* June 4, 1991.

David B. Kopel and Stephen D'Andrilli, "The Swiss and Their Guns," *American Rifleman,* February 1990.

Robert Emmet Long, ed., *Gun Control.* New York: H.W. Wilson, 1989.

Greg Lucas, "State Gun Laws in Spotlight," *San Francisco Chronicle,* March 30, 1991.

Michael Newton, *Armed and Dangerous.* Cincinnati, OH: Writer's Digest Books, 1990.

Lee Nisbet, ed., *The Gun Control Debate: You Decide.* Buffalo, NY: Prometheus Books, 1990.

Patrick W. O'Carroll et al., "Preventing Homicide: An Evaluation of the Efficacy of a Detroit Handgun Ordinance," *The American Journal of Public Health,* May 1991.

Noel Perrin, *Giving Up the Gun: Japan's Reversion to the Sword, 1543-1879.* Boston: David R. Godine, 1979.

Alex Prud'homme, "A Blow to the N.R.A.," *Time,* May 20, 1991.

Mark A. Siegel, Nancy P. Jacobs, and Carol R. Foster, *Gun Control: Protecting Rights or Protecting People?* Buffalo, NY: Prometheus Books, 1991.

Paul Trachtman, *The Gunfighters.* New York: Time-Life Books, 1974.

James B. Trefethen, *Americans and Their Guns.* Harrisburg, PA: Stackpole Books, 1967.

U.S. News & World Report, "Should More Limits Be Placed on Guns?" April 10, 1989.

Daniel W. Webster, C. Patrick Chaulk, Stephen P. Teret, and Garen J. Wintemute, "Reducing Firearm Injuries," *Issues in Science and Technology*, Spring 1991.

Chris Wood, "Violent Land: The Question of Whether Tighter Control of Guns Will Help Stem a Tide of Crime," *Maclean's,* June 10, 1991.

Franklin E. Zimring and Gordon Hawkins, *The Citizen's Guide to Gun Control.* New York: Macmillan, 1987.

Index

About the Author

Neal Bernards is a writer currently living in San Francisco. He received his bachelor of arts degree in writing from Bethel College in St. Paul, Minnesota. Bernards has written six books and edited numerous others. This is his first for Lucent Books.

Picture Credits

Photos supplied by Research Plus, Inc., Mill Valley, California

Cover photo by FPG, International
AP Newsfeatures Photo, 61
AP/Wide World Photos, 26, 31, 32, 36, 52, 54, 75, 80, 82, 86
The Bettmann Archive, 6, 11, 14, 67, 72, 74, 76, 77
Library of Congress, 8, 10, 12, 13, 15, 16, 18, 40, 42, 43, 44, 70, 71
Hollywood Book & Poster, 21
Prints Old & Rare, 17
Reuters/Bettmann, 25, 64
UPI/Bettmann, 22, 33, 46, 49, 68